TARTS

TARTS

40 SUPERB RECIPES FOR SWEET & SAVORY TARTS

This is a Parragon Publishing Book
This edition published in 2006

Parragon Publishing
Queen Street House
4 Queen Street
Bath BA1 1HE, UK

Copyright © Parragon Books Ltd 2004

ISBN: 1-40547-520-X

Printed in China

Design concept by Fiona Roberts
Produced by the Bridgewater Book Company Ltd
Photographer: David Jordan
Home Economist: Jacqueline Bellefontaine

Notes for the Reader

This book uses imperial, metric, or US cup measurements. Follow the same units of
measurement throughout; do not mix imperial and metric. All spoon measurements are
level: teaspoons are assumed to be 5 ml, and tablespoons are assumed to be 15 ml.
Unless otherwise stated, milk is assumed to be whole, eggs and individual vegetables
such as potatoes are medium, and pepper is freshly ground black pepper. Recipes using
raw or very lightly cooked eggs should be avoided by infants, the elderly, pregnant women,
convalescents, and anyone suffering from an illness.

Picture acknowledgment

The Bridgewater Book Company would like to thank Michelle Garrett/Corbis for permission
to reproduce copyright material for the endpapers.

contents

Introduction   6

An Individual Approach   8

The Art of the Tart   28

Fruitful   48

Sweet Indulgence   74

Index   96

Introduction

Tarts are a food of infinite variety and possibility, which can be simple and satisfying or elegant and refined—either way they are always a pleasure to make and eat.

This book contains a collection of tarts for every occasion, whether an intensely flavored two-bite morsel with a cocktail or a deeply impressive tart of fine sophistication. The tart is the simplest and most self-contained form of food and can be dressed up or down. Being eminently portable, it makes a perfect choice for a picnic and is never out of place, even at a celebration dinner party. A tart is always appropriate, whatever the occasion.

Making dough

The following tips will help make your dough a success every time:

• Allow a little more butter and flour than the amount stated in the recipe, extra flour for rolling out the dough, and a little additional butter to grease the tart pan.

• Always roll out the dough and line the pan before chilling, as this will stop the dough from shrinking. In this way you can trim the dough edges before baking to give a neat finishing edge. Always chill dough before cooking.

• Keep the raw dough trimmings to plug any cracks or small holes, which may appear after baking the tart blind. Simply press a little of the raw dough into the crack and the heat of the cooked pastry will fix it in place.

• Preheat the oven with a heavy baking sheet in it on which the tart shell can be placed. This will cook the dough better and make it easier to get the tart in and out of the oven.

• To bake blind, use parchment paper, which you can scrunch up and then smooth out to fit into the tart snugly.

• All the recipes use large eggs.

• The butter and water for the dough should always be as cold as possible and the flour should always be sifted.

• If not using a food processor simply sift the flour and salt into a large bowl and rub in the butter by hand.

• Almost all the large tarts in this book could be adapted to make six or eight individual tarts.

• Pie dough can be made in advance, frozen, then thawed before use.

The possibilities are endless, not only for the filling but also for the pie dough: you can add a whole variety of ingredients to a basic pie dough to enhance and complement the filling—herbs, spices, and cheese are great additions to savory tarts and make the pie dough every bit as important as what it holds. Tarts are also superb if you are planning ahead, as a pastry shell can be made in advance and frozen until needed.

You will find a wide variety of tarts here, sweet and savory, large and small, but above all, smart, sophisticated, and modern.

Individual tartlets served as a first course or light lunch are something rather special. A little more labor-intensive than a single large tart, they are more than worth the trouble as they look fabulous and always impress. One of the advantages of tart-making is that the pie dough can be made then either chilled, frozen, or cooked ahead of time, which gives great flexibility. Small tartlets can be thawed, filled, and cooked in minutes.

Canapé or hors d'oeuvre-type tartlets can be made ahead of time and look pretty presented on a large tray. Once you have made your pastry shells you can let your imagination run wild and fill them with a wonderful mixture of fillings—a great opportunity to create new, unexpected, and imaginative flavor combinations.

AN INDIVIDUAL APPROACH

With smaller tarts the pie dough works as a background to the fillings so it needs to be crisp but also substantial enough to be held in the hand without crumbling. This is most important when making tartlets for parties. The fillings for the tartlets must not make the pie dough soggy so the tartlets must either be baked with their filling and left to go cold or the shells baked ahead, with their filling added just before serving.

MAKES 12 TARTLETS
PIE DOUGH
1½ cups all-purpose flour
pinch of salt
3½ oz/100 g cold butter, cut
   into pieces
cold water

FILLING
1 large red bell pepper or bottled
   pimiento
3½ oz/100 g chorizo dulce sausage,
   chopped into small pieces
pinch of sweet smoked paprika

salt and pepper
2–3 tbsp tomato paste
generous 1 cup heavy cream
½ tsp saffron threads
2 egg yolks

Catalan Pimiento Tartlets

Using a muffin pan rather than an ordinary tartlet pan makes for decent-size tartlets. The dough tends to shrink less as you can bake the tartlet shells blind before adding the filling. If you don't want to bake the tartlets blind put the lined pan in the freezer for 30 minutes before cooking.

• Lightly grease a 3-inch/7.5-cm, 12-hole muffin pan. Sift the flour and salt into a food processor, add the butter, and process until the mixture resembles fine bread crumbs. Tip the mixture into a large bowl and add a little cold water, just enough to bring the dough together. Turn out onto a floured counter and cut the dough in half. Roll out the first piece and cut out 6 x 3½-inch/9-cm circles. Take each circle and roll out to 4¾ inches/12 cm diameter and line the muffin holes, pressing to fit. Repeat with the remaining dough. Line the dough with parchment paper and dried beans and then put into the refrigerator to chill for 30 minutes. Meanwhile, preheat the oven to 400°F/200°C.

• While the dough is chilling, either broil or roast the red bell pepper whole until the skin has blackened and the flesh is soft. Let cool slightly and peel, discarding the seeds and stalk, then slice the bell pepper into thinnish strands (if using bottled pimiento simply drain and slice). Heat a nonstick skillet and cook the chorizo sausage until just browning, add the paprika and season with salt and pepper. Stir for about 1 minute, then remove from the heat.

• Remove the muffin pan from the refrigerator and bake the tartlets blind for 10 minutes in the preheated oven, then carefully remove the paper and beans.

• Spoon a little tomato paste into each tartlet and divide the red bell pepper and chorizo between them. Put the cream and saffron into a small pan and heat to just below simmering point. Beat the egg yolks in a bowl and pour the hot cream over them, whisking to combine. Divide the filling between the tartlets and bake for 10–15 minutes, until just set.

MAKES 6 TARTLETS

PIE DOUGH

generous ¾ cup all-purpose flour

pinch of salt

2½ oz/75 g cold butter, cut into

    pieces

cold water

FILLING

½ cup sour cream

1 tsp creamed horseradish

½ tsp lemon juice

1 tsp Spanish capers, chopped

salt and pepper

3 egg yolks

7 oz/200 g smoked salmon trimmings

bunch fresh dill, chopped

Smoked Salmon, Dill, and Horseradish Tartlets

Other herbs can be used instead of dill—tarragon, lemon balm, or cilantro would all work well. For a very special occasion you could add ½ tsp sour cream, 1 tsp black lumpfish caviar, and a little sprig of dill to each tart just before serving.

• Grease 6 x 3½-inch/9-cm loose-bottom fluted tart pans. Sift the flour and salt into a food processor, add the butter, and process until the mixture resembles fine bread crumbs. Tip the mixture into a large bowl and add a little cold water, just enough to bring the dough together. Turn out onto a floured counter and divide into 6 equal-size pieces. Roll each piece to fit the tart pans. Carefully fit each piece of dough in its shell and press well to fit the pan. Roll the rolling pin over the pan to neaten the edges and trim the excess dough. Cut 6 pieces of parchment paper and fit a piece into each tart, fill with dried beans, and let chill in the refrigerator for 30 minutes. Meanwhile, preheat the oven to 400°F/200°C.

• Bake the tart shells blind for 10 minutes in the preheated oven, then remove the beans and parchment paper.

• Meanwhile, put the sour cream, horseradish, lemon juice, capers, and salt and pepper into a bowl and mix well. Add the egg yolks, the smoked salmon, and the dill and carefully mix again. Divide this mixture between the tart shells and return to the oven for 10 minutes. Let cool in the pans for 5 minutes before serving.

MAKES 12 TARTLETS

PIE DOUGH

1½ cups all-purpose flour

pinch of salt

3½ oz/100 g cold butter, cut into
    pieces

½ tsp confectioners' sugar

cold water

FILLING

2 duck breasts

pinch of salt

2 tbsp butter

1 tbsp olive oil

2 onions, thinly sliced

2 tsp brown sugar

1 tbsp aged balsamic vinegar of
    Modena, plus extra for drizzling

salt and pepper

½ large or 1 small radicchio, trimmed
    and thinly shredded

fresh flatleaf parsley, chopped

Balsamic Duck and Radicchio Tartlets

Ready-cooked Chinese duck would also work well if reheated and shredded. There are many optional garnishes for these tartlets, such as a few thin strips of orange rind, or substitute soy sauce for the balsamic vinegar: let simmer until thick, drizzle over the duck, and top with shredded scallion.

• Grease a 3-inch/7.5-cm, 12-hole muffin pan. Sift the flour and salt into a food processor, add the butter, and process until the mixture resembles fine bread crumbs. Tip the mixture into a large bowl, stir in the sugar, and add a little cold water, just enough to bring the dough together. Turn out onto a floured counter and cut the dough in half. Roll out the first piece and cut out 6 x 3½-inch/9-cm circles. Next take each circle and roll out to 4½ inches/12 cm diameter and fit into the muffin holes, pressing to fit. Do the same with the remaining dough. Put a piece of parchment paper in each hole and then fill with dried beans. Put the pan in the refrigerator to chill for 30 minutes. Meanwhile, preheat the oven to 400°F/200°C.

• Remove the muffin pan from the refrigerator and bake the tartlets blind for 10 minutes in the preheated oven, then carefully remove the paper and beans and return to the oven for an additional 5 minutes. Let cool in the pan until cold, and leave the oven on.

• Wipe the duck breasts, make a series of thin, diagonal cuts in the skin, and rub in a little salt. Place the duck on a rack set over a roasting pan and roast for 25–30 minutes, until crisp. Meanwhile, heat the butter and olive oil in a skillet and add the onions and sugar and cook gently for 20–25 minutes, until soft and slightly caramelized. Add the balsamic vinegar, salt and pepper, and the radicchio and cook for an additional 5 minutes. Remove the duck from the oven and let rest for 5 minutes.

• Place the tartlet shells on a serving dish and spoon in the onion and radicchio. Slice the duck very thinly and divide between the tarts. Sprinkle with the parsley and drizzle with a little more balsamic vinegar. Serve warm.

MAKES 12 TARTLETS

PIE DOUGH

1½ cups all-purpose flour

pinch of salt

3½ oz/100 g cold butter, cut
   into pieces

2 tsp poppy seeds

cold water

FILLING

24 cherry tomatoes

1 tbsp olive oil

2 tbsp unsalted butter

2 tbsp all-purpose flour

generous 1 cup milk

salt and pepper

1¾ oz/50 g sharp Cheddar cheese

scant ½ cup cream cheese

12 fresh basil leaves

Cherry Tomato and Poppy Seed Tartlets

Other ingredients could be added to these tarts, such as half an anchovy in each one before adding the cheese sauce, or a few chopped herbs. Cheese pie dough would also work well: simply add ½ cup finely grated Cheddar or Parmesan cheese to the pie dough before adding the water.

• Lightly grease a 3-inch/7.5-cm, 12-hole muffin pan. Sift the flour and salt into a food processor, add the butter, and process until the mixture resembles fine bread crumbs. Tip the mixture into a large bowl and add the poppy seeds and a little cold water, just enough to bring the dough together. Turn out onto a floured counter and cut the dough in half. Roll out the first piece and cut out 6 x 3½-inch/9-cm circles. Take each circle and roll out to 4½ inches/12 cm diameter and fit into the muffin holes, pressing to fill the holes. Do the same with the remaining dough. Put a piece of parchment paper in each hole and fill with dried beans, then put the pan in the refrigerator to chill for 30 minutes. Meanwhile, preheat the oven to 400°F/200°C.

• Remove the muffin pan from the refrigerator and bake the tartlets blind for 10 minutes in the preheated oven, then remove the paper and beans. Put the tomatoes in an ovenproof dish, drizzle with the olive oil, and roast for 5 minutes.

• Melt the butter in a pan, stir in the flour, and cook for 5–8 minutes. Gradually add the milk, stirring to combine into a white sauce. Cook for an additional 5 minutes. Season well with salt and pepper and stir in the cheeses until well combined. Put 2 tomatoes in each tart shell and spoon in the cheese sauce, then put back into the oven for 15 minutes. Remove from the oven and top each tartlet with a basil leaf.

MAKES 12 TARTLETS
PIE DOUGH
1½ cups all-purpose flour
pinch of celery salt
3½ oz/100 g cold butter, cut
    into pieces
¼ cup walnut halves, chopped
    in a food processor
cold water

FILLING
2 tbsp butter
2 celery stalks, trimmed
    and finely chopped
1 small leek, trimmed
    and finely chopped

scant 1 cup heavy cream, plus
    2 tbsp extra
7 oz/200 g bleu cheese
salt and pepper
3 egg yolks
chopped fresh parsley, to garnish

Bleu Cheese and Walnut Tartlets

This is a good pie dough for savory or sweet dishes. Hazelnuts and pecans work well but don't overchop the nuts: pulse in a food processor just long enough to chop coarsely but fine enough to combine well with the dough.

• Lightly grease a 3-inch/7.5-cm, 12-hole muffin pan. Sift the flour and celery salt into a food processor, add the butter, and process until the mixture resembles fine bread crumbs. Tip the mixture into a bowl and add the walnuts and a little cold water, just enough to bring the dough together. Turn out onto a floured counter and cut the dough in half. Roll out the first piece and cut out 6 x 3½-inch/9-cm circles. Take each circle and roll out to 4½ inches/ 12 cm diameter and fit into the muffin holes, pressing to fill the holes. Do the same with the remaining dough. Put a piece of parchment paper in each hole, fill with dried beans, then put the pan in the refrigerator to chill for 30 minutes. Meanwhile, preheat the oven to 400°F/200°C.

• Remove the muffin pan from the refrigerator and bake the tartlets blind for 10 minutes in the preheated oven, then carefully remove the paper and beans.

• Melt the butter in a skillet and add the celery and leek and cook for 15 minutes, until soft. Add 2 tbsp heavy cream and crumble in the bleu cheese, mix well, and season with salt and pepper. Bring the remaining cream to simmering point in another pan, then pour onto the egg yolks, stirring all the time. Mix in the bleu cheese mixture and spoon into the pastry shells. Bake for 10 minutes, then turn the pan round in the oven and bake for an additional 5 minutes. Let cool in the pan for 5 minutes and sprinkle with parsley.

MAKES 6 TARTLETS

PIE DOUGH

generous ¾ cup all-purpose flour

pinch of salt

2½ oz/75 g cold butter, cut into
    pieces

¼ cup finely grated Parmesan cheese

cold water

FILLING

scant 1½ cups fresh or frozen petits
    pois

2 tbsp unsalted butter

2 shallots, peeled and finely chopped

3½ oz/100 g cooked ham, chopped

3–4 fresh mint leaves, chopped

½ cup sour cream

3 egg yolks

salt and pepper

Pea, Ham, and Sour Cream Tartlets

For a pretty addition to these tarts crack a quail's egg into a small hollow in the filling of each tart before baking. These tarts have quite a delicate summery taste and are a perfect choice for a summer picnic or lunch.

• Grease 6 x 3½-inch/9-cm loose-bottom fluted tart pans. Sift the flour and salt into a food processor, add the butter, and process until the mixture resembles fine bread crumbs. Tip the mixture into a large bowl and add the Parmesan and a little cold water, just enough to bring the dough together. Turn out onto a floured counter and divide into 6 equal-size pieces. Roll each piece to fit the tart pans. Carefully fit each piece of dough in its shell and press well to fit the pan. Roll the rolling pin over the pan to neaten the edges and trim the excess dough. Cut 6 pieces of parchment paper and fit a piece into each tart, fill with dried beans, and let chill in the refrigerator for 30 minutes. Meanwhile, preheat the oven to 400°F/200°C.

• Bake the tart shells blind for 10 minutes in the preheated oven, then remove the beans and parchment paper.

• Meanwhile, cook the peas in boiling water for 3–4 minutes, until just tender, then drain. Melt the butter in a skillet, add the shallots, and cook gently for 10 minutes, then add the ham and cook for an additional 3–5 minutes. Add the peas and chopped mint, remove from the heat, and stir in the sour cream and egg yolks. Season with salt and pepper and divide between the tart shells. Bake for 12–15 minutes.

MAKES 6 TARTLETS
PIE DOUGH
generous ¾ cup all-purpose flour
pinch of salt
2½ oz/75 g cold butter, cut into
    pieces
cold water

FILLING
5 tbsp heavy cream
4 tbsp bottled artichoke paste
salt and pepper
14 oz/400 g canned artichoke
    hearts, drained

12 thin-cut pancetta slices
arugula leaves
1¾ oz/50 g Parmesan or pecorino
    cheese
2 tbsp olive oil, for drizzling

Artichoke and Pancetta Tartlets

Olive paste (tapenade) or pesto can replace the artichoke paste; just stir with the cream and season well with salt and pepper. For a vegetarian version, substitute peperonata (cooked mixed bell pepper strips) or mozzarella cheese for the pancetta.

• Grease 6 x 3½-inch/9-cm loose-bottom fluted tart pans. Sift the flour and salt into a food processor, add the butter, and process until the mixture resembles fine bread crumbs. Tip the mixture into a large bowl and add a little cold water, just enough to bring the dough together. Turn out onto a floured counter and divide into 6 equal-size pieces. Roll each piece to fit the tart pans. Carefully fit each piece of dough in its shell and press well to fit the pan. Roll the rolling pin over the pan to neaten the edges and trim the excess dough. Cut 6 pieces of parchment paper and fit a piece into each tart, fill with dried beans, and let chill in the refrigerator for 30 minutes. Meanwhile, preheat the oven to 400°F/200°C.
• Bake the tart shells for 10 minutes in the preheated oven and then remove the beans and parchment paper.
• Meanwhile, stir the cream and the artichoke paste together and season well with salt and pepper. Divide between the pastry shells, spreading out to cover the base of each tart. Cut each artichoke heart into 3 pieces and divide between the tarts, curl 2 slices of the pancetta into each tart, and bake for 10 minutes. To serve, top each tart with a good amount of arugula then, using a potato peeler, sprinkle shavings of the Parmesan cheese over the tarts, drizzle with olive oil, and serve at once.

MAKES 6 TARTLETS

PIE DOUGH

generous ¾ cup all-purpose flour

pinch of salt

2½ oz/75 g cold butter, cut into
 pieces

½ fresh nutmeg, grated

cold water

FILLING

6 cups baby spinach

2 tbsp butter

salt and pepper

⅔ cup heavy cream

3 egg yolks

4½ oz/125 g feta cheese

scant ⅓ cup pine nuts

Feta and Spinach Tartlets

These tarts are delicious hot served with a tomato and olive salad or as part of a Greek supper. They can also be made with phyllo pastry for an authentic Greek touch.

• Grease 6 x 3½-inch/9-cm loose-bottom fluted tart pans. Sift the flour and salt into a food processor, add the butter, and process until the mixture resembles fine bread crumbs. Tip the mixture into a large bowl and add the nutmeg and a little cold water, just enough to bring the dough together. Turn out onto a floured counter and divide into 6 equal-size pieces. Roll each piece to fit the tart pans. Carefully fit each piece of dough in its shell and press well to fit the pan. Roll the rolling pin over the pan to neaten the edges and trim the excess dough. Cut 6 pieces of parchment paper and fit a piece into each tart, fill with dried beans, and let chill in the refrigerator for 30 minutes. Meanwhile, preheat the oven to 400°F/200°C.

• Bake the tart shells blind for 10 minutes in the preheated oven, then remove the beans and paper.

• Blanch the spinach in boiling water for just 1 minute, then drain, and press to squeeze all the water out. Chop the spinach. Melt the butter in a skillet, add the spinach, and cook gently to evaporate any remaining liquid. Season well with salt and pepper. Stir in the cream and egg yolks. Crumble the feta and divide between the tarts, top with the creamed spinach, and bake for 10 minutes. Sprinkle the pine nuts over the tartlets and cook for an additional 5 minutes.

MAKES 6 TARTLETS
PUFF PASTRY
1⅛ cups all-purpose flour
pinch of salt
6 oz/175 g unsalted butter
about ⅔ cup chilled water
(or use 9 oz/250 g ready-made
    puff pastry)

FILLING
1 large or 2 small eggplants, trimmed
    and thinly sliced
5 tbsp olive oil
3 buffalo mozzarella cheeses, sliced
6 tbsp pesto
black pepper
1 egg yolk
6 slices prosciutto

Eggplant, Pesto, and Prosciutto Tartlets

Homemade puff pastry is not difficult but it is rather time-consuming because of all the chilling time involved. If you do have time it really is worth making your own, although ready-made pastry will work just as well.

• To make the puff pastry sift the flour and salt into a large mixing bowl and rub in 2 tbsp butter. Gradually add the water, just enough to bring the dough together, and knead briefly to form a smooth dough. Wrap the dough in plastic wrap and let chill for 30 minutes. Keep the remaining butter out of the refrigerator and wrap it in a piece of plastic wrap, then shape it into a 1¼-inch/3-cm thick rectangle. Roll out the dough to a rectangle 3 times longer and 1¼ inches/3 cm wider than the butter and place the butter in the center, long-side toward you. Fold over the 2 "wings" of dough to enclose the butter—press down the edges to seal, then turn the dough so the short side faces you. Roll the dough to its original length, fold into 3, turn, and roll again to its original length. Repeat this once more and then rewrap the dough and let chill again for 30 minutes. Remove from the refrigerator and repeat the rolling and turning twice more. Let chill again for 30 minutes. At this point you can freeze the dough until you need it.
• When you are ready to make the tarts, cut the dough into 6, and roll into either circles or rectangles, then place on 2 baking sheets, 3 on each. Preheat the oven to 375°F/190°C.
• Brush the eggplant slices with 2 tbsp of the olive oil and cook briefly in a nonstick skillet, in batches, then arrange the slices neatly overlapping on each dough base, leaving a 1-inch/2.5-cm margin round the edges. Lay the mozzarella slices over the eggplant slices and spoon over the pesto. Drizzle with the remaining olive oil and season with black pepper. Brush the edges of the dough with egg yolk and bake for 15 minutes. Remove from the oven and drape a slice of prosciutto on each tart before serving.

Possibly the easiest of tarts to turn out, the savory main-course tart can be adapted to suit all sorts of occasions. A freeform puff pastry tart taking its inspiration from France or Italy is perfect for a picnic, lunch, or supper as it is substantial and satisfying and can be topped with whatever you have in the pantry and refrigerator. Bottled or canned Italian vegetables such as bell peppers, olives, and artichokes combined with a little cheese and a few fresh herbs on ready-made puff pastry makes a delicious tart. For something more sophisticated, a crisp pastry shell filled with a creamy fish filling makes an easy, impressive dish.

Texture and flavor are particularly important when a tart forms the centerpiece of a meal, and a perfectly executed tart can be the most pleasing of dinners as well as a very satisfying dish to produce.

THE ART OF THE TART

The opportunities to experiment with flavorings for the pie dough are considerable and even if you are simply filling your tart with eggs, bacon, and cheese, adding a little English mustard powder to the pie dough gives an extra dimension. Think around the ingredients and experiment with flavors that complement the filling, but don't be tempted to overdo it, as this should be a subtle addition.

SERVES 6

PIE DOUGH

scant ¾ cup all-purpose flour

pinch of salt

2½ oz/75 g cold butter, cut
   into pieces

cold water

FILLING

10½ oz/300 g prepared white
   and brown crabmeat

1 bunch watercress, washed
   and leaves picked from stems

¼ cup milk

2 large eggs, plus 3 egg yolks

scant 1 cup heavy cream

salt and pepper

½ tsp ground nutmeg

½ bunch fresh chives, snipped

2 tbsp finely grated Parmesan cheese

Crab and Watercress Tart

Other fish could be
substituted for the crab,
such as flaked salmon or a
mixture of lightly cooked
white and smoked fish.
You could also add a few
capers if you like them.

• Lightly grease a 9-inch/22-cm loose-bottom fluted tart pan. Sift the flour and salt into a food processor, add the butter, and process until the mixture resembles fine bread crumbs. Tip the mixture into a large bowl and add a little cold water, just enough to bring the dough together. Turn out onto a floured counter and roll out the dough 3¼ inches/8 cm larger than the pan. Carefully lift the dough into the pan and press to fit. Roll the rolling pin over the pan to neaten the edges and trim the excess dough. Fit a piece of parchment paper into the tart shell, fill with dried beans, and let chill in the refrigerator for 30 minutes. Meanwhile, preheat the oven to 375°F/190°C.

• Remove the pastry shell from the refrigerator and bake blind for 10 minutes in the preheated oven, then remove the beans and paper. Return to the oven for 5 minutes. Remove the pan from the oven and lower the oven temperature to 325°F/160°C.

• Arrange the crabmeat and watercress in the tart pan. Whisk the milk, eggs, and egg yolks together in a bowl. Bring the cream to simmering point in a pan and pour over the egg mixture, whisking all the time. Season with salt, pepper, and nutmeg and stir in the chives. Carefully pour this mixture over the crab and watercress and sprinkle over the Parmesan. Bake for 35–40 minutes, until golden and set. Let the tart stand for 10 minutes before serving.

SERVES 6

PUFF PASTRY

1⅛ cups all-purpose flour

pinch of salt

6 oz/175 g unsalted butter

about ⅔ cup chilled water

(or use 9 oz/250 g ready-made
   puff pastry)

TOPPING

3 tbsp sundried tomato paste

9 oz/250 g ripe vine tomatoes, sliced

5½ oz/150 g cherry tomatoes, cut
   in half

2 sprigs fresh rosemary

2 tbsp extra virgin olive oil

1 tbsp balsamic vinegar

1 egg yolk

4½ oz/125 g Italian sliced salami,
   chopped

salt and pepper

handful thyme sprigs

Triple Tomato Tart

You can use any combination of tomatoes here, including a few strips of sundried tomatoes in oil when you add the salami. A mixture of yellow and red tomatoes looks pretty, or use roasted bell peppers and pine nuts instead of the salami, and add a few slices of soft goat cheese before baking.

• To make the puff pastry sift the flour and salt into a large mixing bowl and rub in 2 tbsp butter. Gradually add the water, just enough to bring the pastry together, and knead briefly to form a smooth dough. Wrap the dough in plastic wrap and let chill for 30 minutes. Keep the remaining butter out of the refrigerator, wrap it in a piece of plastic wrap, and shape it into a 1¼-inch/3-cm thick rectangle. Roll out the dough to a rectangle 3 times longer and 1¼ inches/3 cm wider than the butter and place the butter in the center, long-side toward you. Fold over the 2 "wings" of dough to enclose the butter—press down the edges to seal and then turn the dough so the short side faces you. Roll the dough to its original length, fold into 3, turn, and roll again to its original length. Repeat this once more and then rewrap the dough and let chill again for 30 minutes. Remove from the refrigerator and repeat the rolling and turning twice more. Let chill again for 30 minutes. At this point you can freeze the dough until you need it.

• When you are ready to make your tart, preheat the oven to 375°F/190°C. Roll out the dough to form a rectangle 14 inches/36 cm long and 10 inches/25 cm wide and lift onto a heavy-duty baking sheet. Spread the sundried tomato paste over the dough leaving a 1¼-inch/3-cm margin round the edge. Arrange the vine tomato slices over the tomato paste, sprinkle over the cherry tomato halves, top with the rosemary, and drizzle with 1 tbsp olive oil and the balsamic vinegar. Brush the edges of the dough with the egg yolk and bake for 10 minutes. Sprinkle over the salami and bake for an additional 10–15 minutes.

• Remove the tart from the oven and season with salt and pepper. Drizzle with the remaining oil and sprinkle with the thyme.

SERVES 6

PUFF PASTRY

1⅛ cups all-purpose flour

pinch of salt

6 oz/175 g unsalted butter

about ⅔ cup chilled water

(or use 9 oz/250 g ready-made

    puff pastry)

FILLING

3–4 medium waxy potatoes

10½ oz/300 g fontina cheese,

    cut into cubes

1 red onion, thinly sliced

3 large sprigs fresh rosemary

2 tbsp olive oil

salt and pepper

1 egg yolk

Potato, Fontina, and Rosemary Tart

You can use different cheeses in this tart—Gorgonzola works well—and add a few lardons or bacon pieces. Oregano can replace the rosemary, and you can add a handful of pitted black olives if you wish.

• To make the puff pastry sift the flour and salt into a large mixing bowl and rub in 2 tbsp butter. Gradually add the water, just enough to bring the pastry together, and knead briefly to form a smooth dough. Wrap the dough in plastic wrap and let chill for 30 minutes. Keep the remaining butter out of the refrigerator, wrap it in a piece of plastic wrap, and shape it into a 1¼-inches/3-cm thick rectangle. Roll out the dough to a rectangle 3 times longer and 1¼ inches/3 cm wider than the butter and place the butter in the center, long-side toward you. Fold over the 2 "wings" of dough to enclose the butter—press down the edges to seal and then turn the dough so the short side faces you. Roll the dough to its original length, fold into 3, turn, and roll again to its original length. Repeat this once more, then rewrap the dough and let chill again for 30 minutes. Remove from the refrigerator and repeat the rolling and turning twice more. Let chill again for 30 minutes. At this point you can freeze the dough until you need it.

• Roll the dough into a large circle and place on a baking sheet. Preheat the oven to 375°F/190°C. Peel the potatoes and slice them as thinly as possible, so they are almost transparent—a mandoline is the best utensil for this, if you have one. Arrange the potato slices in a spiral, overlapping the slices to cover the dough and leaving a ¾-inch/2-cm margin round the edge. Arrange the cheese and onion over the potatoes, sprinkle with the rosemary, and drizzle over the olive oil. Season with salt and pepper and brush the edges with the egg yolk. Bake for 25 minutes, until the potatoes are tender and the pastry brown and crisp.

SERVES 6

PIE DOUGH

generous ¾ cup all-purpose flour

pinch of salt

2½ oz/75 g cold butter, cut into
    pieces

cold water

FILLING

½ small butternut squash or 1 slice
    pumpkin, weighing 9 oz/250 g

1 tsp olive oil

generous 1 cup heavy cream

salt and pepper

6 oz/175 g Gorgonzola cheese

2 eggs, plus 1 egg yolk

6–8 fresh sage leaves

Squash, Sage, and Gorgonzola Tart

This tart is best eaten warm. The squash gives it a slight sweetness, which complements the cheese perfectly and makes it popular with children.

• Cut the squash in half and brush the cut side with the oil. Place cut-side up on a baking sheet and bake for 30–40 minutes, until browned and very soft. Let cool. Remove the seeds and scoop out the flesh into a large bowl, discarding the skin.

• Lightly grease a 9-inch/22-cm loose-bottom fluted tart pan. Sift the flour and salt into a food processor, add the butter, and process until the mixture resembles fine bread crumbs. Tip the mixture into a large bowl and add a little cold water, just enough to bring the dough together. Turn out onto a floured counter and roll out the dough 3¼ inches/8 cm larger than the pan. Carefully lift the dough into the pan and press to fit. Roll the rolling pin over the pan to neaten the edges and remove the excess dough from the edges. Fit a piece of parchment paper into the tart shell, fill with dried beans, and let chill in the refrigerator for 30 minutes. Meanwhile, preheat the oven to 375°F/190°C.

• Remove the pastry shell from the refrigerator and bake the tart shell blind for 10 minutes in the preheated oven, then remove the beans and paper. Return to the oven for 5 minutes.

• Mash the squash and mix with half the cream, season with salt and pepper, and spread in the pastry shell. Slice the cheese and lay it on top. Whisk the remaining cream with the eggs and egg yolk and pour the mixture into the tart pan, making sure it settles evenly. Arrange the sage leaves in a circle on the surface. Bake for 30–35 minutes and leave for 10 minutes in the pan before serving.

SERVES 6

PIE DOUGH

scant 1¾ cups all-purpose flour

pinch of salt

4½ oz/125 g cold butter, cut into
    pieces

scant ½ cup grated Parmesan
    cheese

1 egg

cold water

FILLING

2 large yellow zucchini

1 tbsp salt

3 heaping tbsp unsalted butter

1 bunch scallions, trimmed and finely
    sliced

²⁄₃ cup heavy cream

3 large eggs

salt and white pepper

1 small bunch fresh chives, chopped

Yellow Zucchini Tart

This tart has a wonderful
sun-yellow color and is
quite substantial. It makes
a particularly good tart
for a picnic, as it is robust
enough for transporting.
Keep in its pan and
wrap in foil.

• Grease a 10-inch/25-cm loose-bottom tart pan. Sift the flour and salt into a food processor, add the butter, and pulse to combine, then tip into a large bowl. Add the Parmesan cheese and mix together the egg and water. Add most of the egg mixture and work to a soft dough, using more egg mixture if needed. Turn out onto a floured counter and roll out the dough 3¼ inches/8 cm larger than the pan. Carefully lift the dough into the pan and press to fit. Roll the rolling pin over the pan to neaten the edges and trim the excess dough. Fit a piece of parchment paper into the tart shell, fill with dried beans, and let chill in the refrigerator for 30 minutes. Meanwhile, preheat the oven to 400°F/200°C.

• Bake the tart shell blind for 15 minutes in the preheated oven, then remove the beans and paper and bake for an additional 5 minutes. Remove from the oven and let cool. Lower the oven temperature to 350°F/180°C.

• Meanwhile, grate the zucchini and put in a strainer with 1 tbsp salt. Let drain for 20 minutes, then rinse and put in a clean dish towel, squeezing all the moisture from the zucchini. Keep dry.

• Melt the butter in a wide skillet, sauté the scallions until soft, then add the zucchini and cook over medium heat for 5 minutes, until any liquid has evaporated. Let cool slightly. Whisk the cream and eggs together with the salt and pepper and chives. Spoon the zucchini into the tart shell and pour in the cream mixture, making sure it settles properly, and bake for 30 minutes. Serve hot or cold.

SERVES 6
PIE DOUGH
scant 1¾ cups all-purpose flour
pinch of salt
4½ oz/125 g cold butter, cut into
    pieces
½ cup grated Parmesan cheese
1 egg
cold water

FILLING
11 oz/300 g selection of baby spring
    vegetables, such as carrots,
    asparagus, peas, fava beans,
    scallions, corn cobs, leeks
generous 1¼ cups heavy cream

4½ oz/125 g sharp Cheddar cheese,
    grated
2 eggs plus 3 egg yolks
salt and pepper
handful fresh tarragon and flatleaf
    parsley, chopped

Spring Vegetable Tart

Use only the most tender of young vegetables for this tart. If they are really small, you can leave them whole. A few slices of soft goat cheese could be added just before baking.

• Grease a 10-inch/25-cm loose-bottom tart pan. Sift the flour and salt into a food processor, add the butter, and pulse to combine, then tip into a large bowl and add the Parmesan cheese. Mix the egg and water together in a small bowl. Add most of the egg mixture and work into a soft dough, using more egg mixture if needed. Turn out onto a floured counter and roll out the dough 3¼ inches/8 cm larger than the pan. Carefully lift the dough into the pan and press to fit. Roll the rolling pin over the pan to neaten the edges and trim the excess dough. Fit a piece of parchment paper into the tart shell, fill with dried beans, and let chill in the refrigerator for 30 minutes. Meanwhile, preheat the oven to 400°F/200°C.

• Bake the tart shell blind for 15 minutes in the preheated oven, then remove the beans and paper and bake for an additional 5 minutes. Remove from the oven and let cool. Lower the oven temperature to 350°F/180°C.

• Prepare the vegetables by trimming and peeling where necessary, then cut them into bite-size pieces and blanch in boiling water. Drain and let cool. Bring the cream to simmering point in a pan. Place the cheese, eggs, and egg yolks in a heatproof bowl and pour the warm cream over the mixture. Stir to combine, season well with salt and pepper, and stir in the herbs. Arrange the vegetables in the tart shell, pour over the cheese filling, and bake for 30–40 minutes, until set. Let cool in the pan for 10 minutes before serving.

SERVES 6

PIE DOUGH

generous ¾ cup all-purpose flour

pinch of salt

2½ oz/75 g cold butter, cut into
    pieces

½ tsp ground cumin

cold water

FILLING

1 tsp vegetable oil

2 tbsp butter

1 tsp garam masala

1 tsp ground coriander

1 tsp ground turmeric

½ tsp ground cumin

½ tsp ground ginger

1 garlic clove, crushed

1 lb 2 oz/500 g onions, thinly sliced

1 tsp brown sugar

2 eggs, plus 2 egg yolks

generous 1 cup heavy cream

salt and pepper

bunch fresh cilantro, chopped

Curried Onion Tart

This tart, with its Indian flavors, is good served with a cooling cucumber raita: stir a little chopped cucumber into plain yogurt, add a little salt, and sprinkle over a few toasted slivered almonds. This recipe also works well for individual tartlets, topped with a little mango chutney before serving.

• Lightly grease a 9-inch/22-cm loose-bottom fluted tart pan. Sift the flour and salt into a food processor, add the butter, and process until the mixture resembles fine bread crumbs. Tip the mixture into a large bowl, sprinkle in the cumin, and a little cold water, just enough to bring the dough together. Turn out onto a floured counter and roll out the dough 3¼ inches/8 cm larger than the pan. Carefully lift the dough into the pan and press to fit. Roll the rolling pin over the pan to neaten the edges and trim the excess dough. Fit a piece of parchment paper into the tart shell, fill with dried beans, and let chill for 30 minutes. Meanwhile, preheat the oven to 375°F/190°C.

• Remove the pastry shell from the refrigerator and bake blind for 10 minutes in the preheated oven, then remove the beans and parchment paper. Return to the oven for 5 minutes.

• Meanwhile, heat the oil and butter in a skillet, stir in the spices, and cook for 2 minutes. Add the garlic, onion, and sugar and cook for 10 minutes, then cover the skillet and cook for an additional 20 minutes, until the onion is very soft. Remove the lid and let the onions color and caramelize slightly. Beat the eggs, egg yolks, and cream together and season with salt and pepper. Spoon the onions into the tart shell and pour in the eggs and cream. Sprinkle some fresh cilantro over the top and bake for 30–35 minutes. Let cool in the pan for 10 minutes, then sprinkle over more cilantro before serving.

SERVES 6

PIE DOUGH

generous ¾ cup all-purpose flour

pinch of salt

2½ oz/75 g cold butter, cut into
   pieces

½ tsp English mustard powder

1 egg yolk

cold water

FILLING

9 oz/250 g undyed smoked haddock

1¼ cups milk

1 bay leaf

2 tbsp butter

2 tbsp all-purpose flour

½ tsp ground nutmeg

white pepper

4½ oz/125 g Gruyère cheese, grated

2 eggs, separated

Smoked Haddock and Gruyère Soufflé Tart

This impressive looking tart can be made simply with cheese, instead of the haddock. Use a combination of your favorite cheeses or use a little chopped cooked ham and some soft herbs instead of the fish.

• Lightly grease a 9-inch/22-cm loose-bottom fluted tart pan. Sift the flour and salt into a food processor, add the butter, and process until the mixture resembles fine bread crumbs. Tip the mixture into a large bowl and sprinkle in the mustard powder. Mix the egg yolk with a little cold water and add a little of the mixture to the bowl, just enough to bring the dough together. Turn out onto a floured counter and roll out the dough 3¼ inches/8 cm larger than the pan. Carefully lift the dough into the pan and press to fit. Roll the rolling pin over the pan to neaten the edges and trim the excess dough. Fit a piece of parchment paper into the tart shell, fill with dried beans, and let chill in the refrigerator for 30 minutes. Meanwhile, preheat the oven to 375°F/190°C.

• Remove the pastry shell from the refrigerator and bake blind for 10 minutes in the preheated oven, then remove the beans and parchment paper. Return to the oven for 5 minutes.

• Meanwhile, put the haddock, milk, and bay leaf in a shallow skillet, bring to simmering point, and poach the fish for 3–5 minutes, until just cooked. Remove from the heat, discard the bay leaf, and carefully lift out the fish, reserving the milk. Let the fish cool slightly and flake, discarding any bones or skin. Increase the oven temperature to 400°F/200°C.

• Melt the butter in a medium pan and stir in the flour to make a roux. Gradually add the reserved cooking milk, stirring well to combine, and cook for 5 minutes, until thickened. Stir in the nutmeg and pepper and then the cheese. Remove the sauce from the heat, stir in the egg yolks and fish, and let cool slightly. Meanwhile, whisk the egg whites until stiff, then fold quickly and lightly into the fish mixture. Immediately pour into the tart shell and bake for 15 minutes, until puffed up and browned. Remove the tart from the oven and let rest for 10 minutes before serving.

SERVES 6

PUFF PASTRY

1⅛ cups all-purpose flour

pinch of salt

6 oz/175 g unsalted butter

about ⅔ cup chilled water

(or use 9 oz/250 g ready-made

   puff pastry)

TOPPING

1 lb 2 oz/500 g goat cheese,

   such as chèvre, sliced

3–4 sprigs fresh thyme,

   leaves picked from stalks

scant ⅓ cup black olives, pitted

1¾ oz/50 g tinned anchovies

   in olive oil

1 tbsp olive oil

salt and pepper

1 egg yolk

Goat Cheese and Thyme Tart

Serve this tart hot, straight from the oven, and sprinkle over arugula leaves or shredded radicchio, drizzle with olive oil, and sprinkle chopped walnuts over the top.

• To make the puff pastry sift the flour and salt into a large mixing bowl and rub in 2 tbsp butter. Gradually add the water, just enough to bring the pastry together, and knead briefly to form a smooth dough. Wrap the dough in plastic wrap and let chill for 30 minutes. Keep the remaining butter out of the refrigerator, wrap it in a piece of plastic wrap, and shape it into a 1¼-inch/3-cm thick rectangle. Roll out the dough to a rectangle 3 times longer and 1¼ inches/3 cm wider than the butter and place the butter in the center, long-side toward you. Fold over the 2 "wings" of dough to enclose the butter—press down the edges to seal and then turn the dough so the short side faces you. Roll the dough to its original length, fold into 3, turn, and roll again to its original length. Repeat this once more and then rewrap the dough and let chill again for 30 minutes. Remove from the refrigerator and repeat the rolling and turning twice more, chilling again for 30 minutes. At this point you can freeze the dough until you need it.

• Roll the dough into a large circle or rectangle and place on a baking sheet. Preheat the oven to 375°F/190°C.

• Arrange the cheese slices on the dough, leaving a 1-inch/2.5-cm margin round the edge. Sprinkle the thyme and olives, and arrange the anchovies, over the cheese. Drizzle over the olive oil. Season well and brush the edges of the dough with the egg yolk. Bake for 20–25 minutes, until the cheese is bubbling and the pastry is browned.

There are an infinite number of possibilities with fruit tarts. The fruit specified in the recipe can almost always be substituted for your own favorite fruit. For fall and winter, fruits such as apples lend themselves to delicious treatments such as Tarte Tatin. Pears work particularly well with more robust pie dough and comforting accompaniments such as crème anglaise. Summer fruit tarts with crisp buttery pie dough and soft fruits are a wonderful treat and can be made into a dramatic centerpiece for a summer lunch or dinner, while tropical fruits look beautiful and taste delightfully sweet.

As we now have a broader choice of exotic fruits, the possibilities for creative tart-making are endless. Experiment with lesser-known fruit such as quince, which has a unique fragrance and flavor and can often be used where apples and pears are specified.

FRUITFUL

The easiest of tarts is a pastry shell baked blind, then filled with sweetened whipped cream and topped with berries or poached fruits. Take into account color contrasts in presenting these tarts—the velvety purple of blueberries looks wonderful with the bright orange of mango or papaya, and the jewellike colors of red currants or pomegranate seeds are perfectly set off against cream-filled chocolate pie dough.

SERVES 6

PIE DOUGH

2¼ cups all-purpose flour

pinch of salt

6 oz/175 g unsalted butter

¼ cup superfine sugar

cold water

FILLING

1 lb 10 oz/750 g blackberries

6 tbsp golden superfine sugar

1 tbsp cassis

5 tsp semolina

1 egg white

TO SERVE

generous 1 cup heavy cream

1 tbsp cassis

fresh mint leaves

Bramble Tart with Cassis Cream

This can also be made with a mixture of berries: mix some raspberries, strawberries, or slices of ripe plum or peach in with the blackberries. Use cassis or a non-alcoholic blackberry-flavored cordial. Also good served with ice cream.

• To make the pie dough, sift the flour and salt into a large bowl and rub in the butter. Stir in the sugar and add enough cold water to bring the dough together, then wrap in plastic wrap and let chill for 30 minutes.

• Meanwhile, rinse and pick over the blackberries, then put in a bowl with 4 tbsp of the sugar and cassis, stirring to coat. Preheat the oven to 400°F/200°C.

• Roll out the dough to a large circle, handling carefully because it is quite a soft dough. Leave the edges ragged and place on a baking sheet. Sprinkle the dough with the semolina, leaving a good 2½-inch/6-cm edge. Pile the fruit into the center and brush the edges of the dough with the egg white. Fold in the edges of the dough to overlap and enclose the fruit, making sure to press together the dough in order to close any gaps. Brush with the remaining egg white, sprinkle with the remaining sugar, and bake for 25 minutes.

• To serve, whip the cream until it starts to thicken and stir in the cassis. Serve the tart hot, straight from the oven, with a good spoonful of the cassis cream and decorated with mint leaves.

SERVES 6

PIE DOUGH

generous ¾ cup all-purpose flour

pinch of salt

2½ oz/75 g cold butter, cut into
    pieces

cold water

FILLING

3 lb/1.3 kg Pippin or other firm,
    sweet apples, peeled and cored

1 tsp lemon juice

3 heaping tbsp butter

½ cup superfine sugar

1 cup granulated sugar

⅓ cup cold water

⅔ cup heavy cream

confectioners' sugar, to dust

Toffee Apple Tart

This tart would also work well with other fruit, such as pears or quinces, or as individual tartlets, each one containing an apricot or a few apple slices smothered in the toffee sauce.

• Lightly grease a 9-inch/22-cm loose-bottom fluted tart pan. Sift the flour and salt into a food processor, add the butter, and process until the mixture resembles fine bread crumbs. Tip the mixture into a large bowl and add the cold water to bring the dough together. Turn out onto a floured counter and roll out the dough 3¼ inches/8 cm larger than the pan. Carefully lift the dough into the pan and press to fit. Roll the rolling pin over the pan to neaten the edges and trim the excess dough. Fit a piece of parchment paper into the tart shell, fill with dried beans, and let chill in the refrigerator for 30 minutes. Meanwhile, preheat the oven to 375°F/190°C.

• Remove the pastry shell from the refrigerator and bake blind for 10 minutes in the preheated oven, then remove the beans and paper. Return to the oven for 5 minutes.

• Meanwhile, take 4 apples, cut each one into 8 pieces and toss in the lemon juice. Melt the butter in a skillet and sauté the apple pieces until just starting to caramelize and brown on the edges. Remove from the skillet and let cool.

• Slice the remaining apples thinly, put them in a pan with the superfine sugar, and cook for about 20–30 minutes, until soft. Spoon the cooked, sliced apple into the pastry shell and arrange the reserved apple pieces on top in a circle. Bake for 30 minutes.

• Put the granulated sugar and water in a pan and heat until the sugar dissolves. Boil to form a caramel. Remove from the heat and add the cream, stirring constantly to combine into toffee. Remove the tart from the oven, pour the toffee over the apples, and let chill for 1 hour. When ready to serve sift a little confectioners' sugar over the tart. Serve with thick cream.

SERVES 6

COCONUT PIE DOUGH

1½ cups all-purpose flour

pinch of salt

4½ oz/125 g cold butter, cut into
  pieces

scant ½ cup dry unsweetened
  coconut

1 tbsp confectioners' sugar

cold water

FILLING

3 lemon grass stalks

generous 1½ cups heavy cream

4 egg yolks

½ cup golden superfine sugar

2 pieces or ¼ oz/6 g fine leaf gelatin

1 large ripe mango or 2 small
  Alphonso mangoes

1–2 tsp confectioners' sugar

Lemon Grass and Mango Tart

This tart can be served as a simple uncaramelized lemon grass tart, without the mango, or you can substitute other exotic fruits or berries. Another option is to dispense with the fruit and brûlé the top instead.

• Finely chop the lemon grass into small pieces or finely grind in a food processor, put in a pan with the cream, and bring to a boil. Remove from the heat, cover, and let infuse for 1 hour.

• Lightly grease a 9-inch/22-cm loose-bottom fluted tart pan. Sift the flour and salt into a food processor, add the butter, and process until the mixture resembles fine bread crumbs. Tip the mixture into a large bowl, stir in the coconut and sugar, and add a little cold water, just enough to bring the dough together. Turn out onto a floured counter and roll out the dough 3¼ inches/8 cm larger than the pan. Carefully lift the dough into the pan and press to fit. Roll the rolling pin over the pan to neaten the edges and trim the excess dough. Fit a piece of parchment paper into the tart shell, fill with dried beans, and let chill in the refrigerator for 30 minutes. Meanwhile, preheat the oven to 375°F/190°C.

• Remove the pastry shell from the refrigerator and bake blind for 15 minutes in the preheated oven, then remove the beans and paper. Return to the oven for 10 minutes, then remove and let cool completely.

• Whisk together the egg yolks and sugar. Strain the cream into a clean pan to remove the lemon grass and whisk in the eggs and sugar. Place on low heat and cook until slightly thickened. Meanwhile, soften the gelatin in a little cold water for 2–3 minutes, then lift out of the water and stir into the hot cream. When the gelatin has dissolved remove the pan from the heat and let cool. Pour the cream mixture into the cold tart shell and let chill for 3–4 hours.

• When you are ready to serve, peel, seed, and thinly slice the mango and arrange randomly over the filling to cover the surface. Sprinkle with confectioners' sugar and caramelize with a blowtorch.

SERVES 6

PUFF PASTRY

1⅛ cups all-purpose flour

pinch of salt

6 oz/175 g unsalted butter

about ⅔ cup chilled water

(or use 9 oz/250 g ready-made
   puff pastry)

FILLING

6–8 just ripe peaches

scant ½ cup golden superfine sugar

3 heaping tbsp unsalted butter

3 pieces preserved ginger in syrup,
   chopped

1 tbsp ginger syrup from the
   preserved ginger jar

1 egg, beaten

Peach and Preserved Ginger Tarte Tatin

This is a modern take on the traditional apple Tarte Tatin. You can use other fruits—plums, apples, and pears all work well. Puff pastry is particularly delicious but basic pie dough or phyllo could also be used.

• To make the puff pastry sift the flour and salt into a large mixing bowl and rub in 2 tbsp butter. Gradually add the water, just enough to bring the pastry together, and knead briefly to form a smooth dough. Wrap the dough in plastic wrap and let chill for 30 minutes. Keep the remaining butter out of the refrigerator, wrap it in a piece of plastic wrap, and shape it into a 1¼-inches/3-cm thick rectangle. Roll out the dough to a rectangle 3 times longer and 1¼ inches/3 cm wider than the butter and place the butter in the center, long-side toward you. Fold over the 2 "wings" of dough to enclose the butter—press down the edges to seal, then turn the dough so the short side faces you. Roll the dough to its original length, fold into 3, turn, and roll again to its original length. Repeat this once more, then rewrap the dough and let chill again for 30 minutes. Remove from the refrigerator and repeat the rolling and turning twice more, then let chill again for 30 minutes. At this point you can freeze the dough until you need it.

• Preheat the oven to 375°F/190°C. Plunge the peaches into boiling water, then let drain and peel. Cut each in half. Put the sugar in a 10-inch/25-cm heavy, ovenproof skillet and heat it gently until it caramelizes. Don't stir, just shake the skillet if necessary. Once the sugar turns a dark caramel color, remove from the heat, and drop 2 tbsp of the butter into it.

• Place the peaches cut-side up on top of the caramel, packing them as close together as possible, and tucking the preserved ginger pieces into any gaps. Dot with the remaining butter and drizzle with the ginger syrup. Return to gentle heat while you roll out the dough in a circle larger than the skillet you are using. Drape the dough over the peaches and tuck it in well round the edges, brush with the beaten egg, and bake for 20–25 minutes, until the pastry is browned and puffed up. Remove from the oven and let rest for 5 minutes, then invert onto a serving plate and serve with thick cream or ice cream.

SERVES 6

PIE DOUGH

1 1/8 cups all-purpose flour

1 tsp confectioners' sugar

pinch of salt

3 1/2 oz/100 g cold butter, cut
    into pieces

1 egg yolk

finely grated rind of 1/2 lemon

cold water

FILLING

2 large eggs

scant 1/2 cup superfine sugar

3 1/2 oz/100 g unsalted butter, cut
    into cubes

juice of 2–3 lemons (1/2 cup)

1 1/2 cups fresh blueberries

1 tbsp cassis (optional)

1 tbsp confectioners' sugar (optional)

TO DECORATE

finely grated rind of the lemons
    used in the filling

confectioners' sugar

Lemon Curd and Blueberry Tart

To make orange curd, substitute orange juice and grated orange rind for the lemon juice and rind. Spread over the tart shell and top with peeled orange slices drizzled with a little orange flower water.

• This tart looks very pretty made in a fluted loose-bottom rectangular tart pan, 13 x 4 inches/33 x 10 cm wide, or a 9-inch/22-cm round pan. Make the lemon curd filling first. Put the eggs in a heatproof bowl and whisk in the sugar. Add the cubed butter and the lemon juice and place over a pan of simmering water, whisking constantly until the ingredients are well combined. Continue stirring for 10 minutes, until the mixture thickens. Remove from the heat and let cool. Keep covered until needed.

• To make the pie dough put the flour, sugar, and salt in a food processor, add the butter, and process until the mixture resembles bread crumbs. Tip into a large bowl, add the egg yolk and lemon rind, and bring the dough together, adding a little cold water if necessary. Turn out onto a floured counter and roll out to 3 1/4 inches/8 cm larger than the pan. Carefully lift the dough into the pan and press to fit. Roll the rolling pin over the pan to neaten the edges and trim the excess dough. Fit a piece of parchment paper into the tart shell, fill with dried beans, and let chill in the refrigerator for 30 minutes. Meanwhile, preheat the oven to 375°F/190°C.

• Remove the pastry shell from the refrigerator and bake the tart shell blind for 15 minutes in the preheated oven, then remove the beans and paper. Return to the oven for 10 minutes, then remove and let cool completely. Spoon the lemon curd into the tart shell and top with the blueberries. (If you wish, you can poach the blueberries with the cassis and sugar until glossy. Just before the berries start to burst, let cool completely, then spoon over the curd.) Top with the finely grated lemon rind and a little sifted confectioners' sugar.

SERVES 6

PIE DOUGH

generous ¾ cup all-purpose flour

2 tsp unsweetened cocoa

2 tsp confectioners' sugar

pinch of salt

2½ oz/75 g cold butter, cut into
    pieces

1 egg yolk

ice-cold water

FILLING

½ punnet each black currants,
    red currants, and white currants

seeds of 1 large pomegranate

6 egg yolks

scant ⅜ cup superfine sugar

2½ cups heavy cream

1 vanilla bean, split and the seeds
    scraped out

Jewel Berry Tart

Add confectioners'
sugar and pomegranate
molasses or cassis to the
fruits before topping the
tart and sift confectioners'
sugar over the berries
before serving.

• Grease a 9-inch/22-cm loose-bottom fluted tart pan. Sift the flour, cocoa, confectioners' sugar, and salt into a food processor, add the butter, and process until the mixture resembles fine bread crumbs. Tip the mixture into a large bowl and add the egg yolk plus a little ice-cold water to bring the dough together. Turn out onto a counter dusted with more flour and cocoa and roll out the dough 3¼ inches/8 cm larger than the pan. Carefully lift the dough into the pan and press to fit. Roll the rolling pin over the pan to neaten the edges and trim the excess dough. Fit a piece of parchment paper into the tart shell, fill with dried beans, and let chill in the refrigerator for 30 minutes. Meanwhile, preheat the oven to 375°F/190°C.

• Remove the pastry shell from the refrigerator and bake blind for 15 minutes in the preheated oven, then remove the beans and paper. Return to the oven for 10 minutes, then remove and let cool. Run the tines of a fork along the currant stalks to pick off the currants and mix with the pomegranate seeds. Let chill.

• Whisk the egg yolks with the sugar in a heatproof bowl and place over a pan of simmering water, whisking for 10 minutes, or until the mixture has thickened. In a separate pan bring the heavy cream and the split vanilla bean to a boil, then whisk into the eggs and sugar. Stir constantly for an additional 5–8 minutes.

• Take the filling off the heat and remove the vanilla bean. (The bean can be wiped dry and reused in another recipe). Let cool completely, then pour into the tart shell and let chill for 3–4 hours. When you are ready to serve, pile the jeweled berries over the set filling.

SERVES 6

PIE DOUGH

1⅛ cups all-purpose flour

pinch of salt

3½ oz/100 g cold butter,
    cut into pieces

1 tsp confectioners' sugar

1 egg yolk

cold water

FILLING

½ cup elderberry cordial

¼ cup blush or white wine

1 lb 2 oz/500 g strawberries, hulled

1¼ cups heavy cream

½ tsp vanilla extract

2 tbsp confectioners' sugar

Strawberry and Elderberry Tart

A little confectioners' sugar sifted over the tart just before serving adds an attractive finish. If there isn't enough syrup left for drizzling, mix what you have with a little extra wine and sugar.

• This tart looks very pretty made in a fluted loose-bottom rectangular tart pan, 14 x 5 inches/36 x 13 cm, or a 9-inch/22-cm loose-bottom fluted tart pan. Sift the flour and salt into a food processor, add the butter, and process until the mixture resembles fine bread crumbs. Tip the mixture into a large bowl, stir in the sugar, and add the egg yolk and a little cold water to bring the dough together. Turn out onto a floured counter and roll out the dough 3¼ inches/8 cm larger than the pan. Carefully lift the dough into the pan and press to fit. Roll the rolling pin over the pan to neaten the edges and trim the excess dough. Fit a piece of parchment paper into the tart shell, fill with dried beans, and let chill in the refrigerator for 30 minutes. Meanwhile, preheat the oven to 375°F/190°C.

• Remove the pastry shell from the refrigerator and bake the tart shell blind for 20 minutes in the preheated oven, then remove the beans and paper. Return to the oven for 10 minutes, then remove and let cool completely.

• Bring the cordial and wine to a boil in a small pan and let simmer for 5 minutes, then let cool completely. Cut the strawberries into ½-inch/1-cm slices, place in a bowl, and pour over the elderberry syrup. Let chill until needed. Remove the pastry shell carefully from its pan and transfer to a serving plate.

• Put the cream in a bowl and whisk until starting to thicken, add the vanilla and sugar, and whisk again until thick. Spoon into the tart shell and let chill for 30 minutes. Lift the strawberries from the syrup and arrange them randomly or in a fish-scale pattern over the cream. Serve the elderberry syrup in a small pitcher for drizzling over the tart.

SERVES 6

PIE DOUGH

generous ¾ cup all-purpose flour

pinch of salt

3 oz/75 g cold butter, cut into pieces

1 tsp confectioners' sugar

cold water

FILLING

6 egg yolks

scant ½ cup superfine sugar

2½ cups heavy cream

4 passion fruit

4 tbsp confectioners' sugar

Passion Fruit Brûlée Tart

If you don't have a blowtorch, protect the edges of the pie dough with some foil, preheat the broiler until very hot and brûlé under the broiler. The brûlée topping will soften if the tart is not eaten within an hour. It will lose its crispness but it still tastes delicious.

• Lightly grease a 9-inch/22-cm loose-bottom fluted tart pan. Sift the flour and salt into a food processor, add the butter, and process until the mixture resembles fine bread crumbs. Tip the mixture into a large bowl, stir in the sugar, and add a little cold water, just enough to bring the dough together. Turn out onto a floured counter and roll out the dough 3¼ inches/8 cm larger than the pan. Carefully lift the dough into the pan and press to fit. Roll the rolling pin over the pan to neaten the edges and trim the excess dough. Fit a piece of parchment paper into the tart shell, fill with dried beans, and let chill for 30 minutes. Meanwhile, preheat the oven to 375°F/190°C.

• Remove the pastry shell from the refrigerator and bake blind for 20 minutes in the preheated oven, then remove the beans and paper. Return to the oven for 10 minutes, then remove and let cool completely.

• Whisk the egg yolks with the superfine sugar in a heatproof bowl and place over a pan of simmering water, continuing to whisk for 10 minutes, until the mixture has thickened. In a separate pan bring the heavy cream to a boil, then whisk it into the egg and sugar mixture, and cook for an additional 5–8 minutes, stirring. Remove from the heat and let cool. Cut the passion fruit in half and scoop out the juice and seeds into a bowl. When the filling is cold, stir in the passion fruit juice and seeds, and spoon into the pastry shell. Let chill for 3 hours.

• About 30 minutes before you serve, sprinkle 2 tbsp confectioners' sugar over the filling and blowtorch until melted, then repeat with the remaining sugar and blowtorch again until the sugar is browned and bubbling. Let chill for 20 minutes, until the caramelized topping is crisp.

SERVES 6

PIE DOUGH

generous ¾ cup all-purpose flour

pinch of salt

2½ oz/75 g cold butter, cut into
    pieces

1 tsp confectioners' sugar

cold water

FILLING

2 pieces or ¼ oz/6 g fine leaf gelatin

cold water

scant 1 cup unsweetened coconut
    cream

scant ½ cup superfine sugar

scant 2 cups heavy cream

selection of tropical fruits, such
    as mango, papaya, passion fruit,
    cape gooseberries, pineapple,
    and banana, peeled, prepared,
    and cut into bite-size pieces

Tropical Fruit Tart

Make sure you use plenty of fruit. This is meant to be a decadent dessert and as the coconut cream is quite delicate you need the sweetness of the fruit to complement it. Fresh coconut, pared with a potato peeler, makes a delicious extra topping for this tart.

• Lightly grease a 9-inch/22-cm loose-bottom fluted tart pan. Sift the flour and salt into a food processor, add the butter, and process until the mixture resembles fine bread crumbs. Tip the mixture into a large bowl, stir in the sugar, and add a little cold water, just enough to bring the dough together. Turn out onto a floured counter and roll out the dough 3¼ inches/8 cm larger than the pan. Carefully lift the dough into the pan and press to fit. Roll the rolling pin over the pan to neaten the edges and trim the excess dough. Fit a piece of parchment paper into the tart shell, fill with dried beans, and let chill in the refrigerator for 30 minutes. Meanwhile, preheat the oven to 375°F/190°C.

• Remove the pastry shell from the refrigerator and bake the tart shell blind for 20 minutes in the preheated oven, then remove the beans and paper. Return to the oven for 10 minutes, then remove and let cool completely.

• Soak the gelatin in a little cold water while you heat the coconut cream and superfine sugar in a small pan. When soft, lift the gelatin out of the water and stir into the hot coconut cream until dissolved. Let cool. Whisk the heavy cream until stiff and fold in the cold coconut mixture, spoon into the tart shell, and let chill for 3 hours. Arrange a colorful pile of the fruit on top of the coconut cream.

SERVES 6

PIE DOUGH

generous ¾ cup all-purpose flour

pinch of salt

2½ oz/75 g cold butter, cut into
    pieces

scant ⅓ cup ground almonds

cold water

FILLING

6 figs

½ cup superfine sugar

2½ cups water

1 lb 2 oz/500 g ricotta cheese

4 egg yolks

½ tsp vanilla extract

2 tbsp flower honey, plus 1 tsp
    for drizzling

Fig, Ricotta, and Honey Tart

If the figs are very ripe you could skip the poaching process: simply slice the figs and cover the surface of the tart completely, drizzling with honey.

• Lightly grease a 9-inch/22-cm loose-bottom fluted tart pan. Sift the flour and salt into a food processor, add the butter, and process until the mixture resembles fine bread crumbs. Tip the mixture into a large bowl, stir in the almonds, and add a little cold water, just enough to bring the dough together. Turn out onto a floured counter and roll out the dough 3¼ inches/8 cm larger than the pan. Carefully lift the dough into the pan and press to fit. Roll the rolling pin over the pan to neaten the edges and trim the excess dough. Fit a piece of parchment paper into the tart shell, fill with dried beans, and let chill for 30 minutes. Meanwhile, preheat the oven to 375°F/190°C.

• Remove the pastry shell from the refrigerator and bake the tart shell blind for 15 minutes in the preheated oven, then remove the beans and paper. Return to the oven for 5 minutes.

• Put the figs, half the superfine sugar, and the water in a pan and bring to a boil. Poach gently for 10 minutes, drain, and let cool. Drain any liquid from the ricotta and stir in the egg yolks and vanilla extract, add the remaining sugar and the honey, and mix well. Spoon into the tart shell and bake for 30 minutes. Remove from the oven and, when you are ready to serve, cut the figs in half lengthwise and arrange on the tart, cut-side up. Drizzle with the extra honey and serve at once.

SERVES 6

PUFF PASTRY

1⅛ cups all-purpose flour

pinch of salt

6 oz/175 g cold butter

about ⅔ cup chilled water

(or use 9 oz/250 g ready-made

    puff pastry)

TOPPING

1 lb 2 oz/500 g Pippin or

    other firm, sweet apples

4 tbsp superfine sugar

3 heaping tbsp butter

1 egg, beaten

⅔ cup heavy cream

1 tbsp applejack brandy

Apple Galette with Applejack Cream

Almonds work very well with apples so an alternative would be to sprinkle the cooked tart with toasted, slivered almonds and use an almond liqueur instead of the applejack brandy in the cream.

• To make the puff pastry sift the flour and salt into a large mixing bowl and rub in 2 tbsp butter. Gradually add the water, just enough to bring the pastry together, and knead briefly to form a smooth dough. Wrap the dough in plastic wrap and let chill for 30 minutes. Keep the remaining butter out of the refrigerator, wrap in a piece of plastic wrap, and shape it into a 1¼-inch/3-cm thick rectangle. Roll out the dough to a rectangle 3 times longer and 1¼ inches/3 cm wider than the butter and place the butter in the center, long-side toward you. Fold over the 2 "wings" of dough to enclose the butter—press down the edges to seal and then turn the dough so the short side faces you. Roll the dough to its original length, fold into 3, turn, and roll again to its original length. Repeat this once more, then rewrap the dough and let chill again for 30 minutes. Remove from the refrigerator and repeat the rolling and turning twice more. Let chill again for 30 minutes. At this point you can freeze the dough until you need it.

• Peel, core, and thinly slice the apples. Heat the sugar and butter in a skillet, add the apples, and cook gently for 10–15 minutes. Let cool. Preheat the oven to 400°F/200°C. Roll out the dough to a large rectangle and place on a baking sheet. Lift the apples from the skillet with a slotted spoon and arrange in neat rows on the dough, leaving a 1¼-inch/3-cm margin round the edge of the dough. Brush the dough with the egg and bake for 30–35 minutes. Reheat the apple butter syrup and reduce until it is thick, then use it to brush over the apples. Whip the cream, stir in the applejack brandy, and let chill. Serve the hot tart with the cold applejack cream.

SERVES 6

PIE DOUGH

generous ¾ cup all-purpose flour

pinch of salt

2½ oz/75 g cold butter, cut into
  pieces

1 tsp confectioners' sugar

cold water

FILLING

2 firm pears, peeled, cored,
  and halved

1 large strip lemon rind

scant 1 cup Marsala

scant 1 cup superfine sugar

generous ⅓ cup water

6 oz/175 g butter

3 eggs

2 cups ground almonds

scant ⅓ cup all-purpose flour

MARSALA SYLLABUB

½ cup Marsala

⅝ cup superfine sugar

1 cinnamon stick

1 cup heavy cream

Poached Pear Tart with Marsala Syllabub

The syllabub could be flavored with applejack brandy or Poire William. It also works well spooned over poached fruits and served with little sweet cookies.

• Lightly grease a 9-inch/22-cm loose-bottom fluted tart pan. Sift the flour and salt into a food processor, add the butter, and process until the mixture resembles fine bread crumbs. Tip the mixture into a large bowl, stir in the sugar, and add a little cold water, just enough to bring the dough together. Turn out onto a floured counter and roll out the dough 3¼ inches/8 cm larger than the pan. Carefully lift the dough into the pan and press to fit. Roll the rolling pin over the pan to neaten the edges and trim the excess dough. Fit a piece of parchment paper into the tart shell, fill with dried beans, and let chill in the refrigerator for 30 minutes. Meanwhile, preheat the oven to 375°F/190°C.

• Remove the pastry shell from the refrigerator and bake blind for 10 minutes in the preheated oven, then remove the beans and paper. Return to the oven for 5 minutes.

• Put the pears, lemon rind, Marsala, 2 tbsp of the sugar, and the water in a pan and bring to a boil. Let simmer for 30 minutes, or until the pears are tender. Leave in the liquid to cool. Slice the pears lengthwise.

• Melt 5½ oz/150 g of the butter. Beat the remaining sugar with the eggs and stir in the melted butter and then the almonds and flour. Pour the almond mixture into the pastry shell and arrange the pear slices in a cartwheel pattern on top. Melt the remaining butter and brush it over the pears. Bake for 25–30 minutes. Meanwhile, put the Marsala, sugar, and cinnamon stick for the syllabub in a pan and let simmer for 5 minutes. Strain and let cool.

• When you are ready to serve, make the syllabub. Put the cooled Marsala in a bowl and gradually whip in the cream with an electric whisk until soft peaks form. Slice the tart and spoon a spoonful of syllabub on each slice.

The tarts in this chapter come into the category of indulgence because of their luxurious fillings and glamorous appearance. The pie dough for these tarts tends to be fairly plain as it is the fillings that are making the statement, but adding an egg yolk to the pie dough will make it richer, while adding $1/8$ cup of very finely ground amaretti cookies will add an almond crunch to the pie dough. One large tart looks impressive in terms of presentation but all the tarts in this chapter can be made as individual tarts.

Sweet tarts are the perfect excuse for decadent fillings and if you are going to town with a rich filling it really is essential to use the best ingredients you can find: semisweet chocolate with the highest cocoa solids content —at least 70% is a must for the Fine Chocolate Tart—and undyed, natural candied cherries for the Florentine Tarts.

SWEET INDULGENCE

These very rich sweet tarts are usually enough served on their own but if you need a little something extra offer chilled heavy cream for pouring.

For a party, make both the semisweet chocolate and the white chocolate tarts and serve with raspberries—a combination that looks very elegant and enticing. For a smart dinner make these as individual small tartlets and give each guest one white and one semisweet chocolate tartlet and a few berries.

SERVES 6

PIE DOUGH

generous ¾ cup all-purpose flour

2 tsp unsweetened cocoa

2 tsp confectioners' sugar

pinch of salt

1¾ oz/50 g cold butter, cut into
    pieces

1 egg yolk

ice-cold water

GANACHE FILLING

7 oz/200 g semisweet chocolate with
    70% cocoa solids

2 tbsp unsalted butter, softened

1 cup heavy cream

1 tsp dark rum (optional)

Fine Chocolate Tart

If liked, sift more unsweetened cocoa over the surface of the tart or, for serious chocoholics, sprinkle curls of chocolate over the surface. A bowl of sour cream is a lovely accompaniment for this tart.

• Lightly grease a 9-inch/22-cm loose-bottom fluted tart pan. Sift the flour, cocoa, confectioners' sugar, and salt into a food processor, add the butter, and process until the mixture resembles fine bread crumbs. Tip the mixture into a large bowl, add the egg yolk, and add a little ice-cold water, just enough to bring the dough together. Turn out onto a counter dusted with more flour and cocoa and roll out the dough 3¼ inches/8 cm larger than the pan. Carefully lift the dough into the pan and press to fit. Roll the rolling pin over the pan to neaten the edges and trim the excess dough. Fit a piece of parchment paper into the tart shell, fill with dried beans, and let chill in the refrigerator for 30 minutes. Meanwhile, preheat the oven to 375°F/190°C.

• Remove the pastry shell from the refrigerator and bake the pastry shell for 15 minutes in the preheated oven, then remove the beans and paper and bake for an additional 5 minutes.

• To make the ganache filling, chop the chocolate and put in a bowl with the softened butter. Bring the cream to a boil, then pour on to the chocolate, stirring well, add the rum (if using) and continue stirring to make sure the chocolate is melted completely. Pour into the pastry shell and let chill for 3 hours.

SERVES 6

PIE DOUGH

generous ¾ cup all-purpose flour

pinch of salt

2½ oz/75 g cold butter, cut into
   pieces

1 tsp confectioners' sugar

cold water

FILLING

1⅛ cups curd cheese

scant ½ cup cream cheese

½ cup heavy cream

2 egg yolks, plus 1 whole egg

2 tbsp superfine sugar

4 tbsp flower honey, plus extra
   for drizzling

crystallized violets or sugared
   rose petals, to decorate

Truffled Honey Tart

Flower honey, such as lavender, works very well in this recipe, as does chestnut honey. Alternative toppings to sprinkle over the tart include pistachios rolled in honey or coarsely crushed honeycomb.

• Lightly grease a 9-inch/22-cm loose-bottom fluted tart pan. Sift the flour and salt into a food processor, add the butter, and process until the mixture resembles fine bread crumbs. Tip the mixture into a large bowl, add the sugar, and a little cold water, just enough to bring the dough together. Turn out onto a counter dusted with more flour and roll out the dough 3¼ inches/8 cm larger than the pan. Carefully lift the dough into the pan and press to fit. Roll the rolling pin over the pan to neaten the edges and trim the excess dough. Fit a piece of parchment paper into the tart shell, fill with dried beans, and let chill in the refrigerator for 30 minutes. Meanwhile, preheat the oven to 375°F/190°C.

• Remove the pastry shell from the refrigerator and bake blind for 10 minutes in the preheated oven, then remove the beans and paper and bake for an additional 5 minutes.

• Mix the curd cheese, cream cheese, and cream together until smooth, then stir in the egg yolks and whole egg plus the sugar and honey until completely smooth. Pour into the pastry shell and bake for 30 minutes. Remove from the oven and let cool in the pan for 10 minutes. Drizzle with more honey and decorate with violets or petals.

SERVES 6

PIE DOUGH

generous ¾ cup all-purpose flour

pinch of salt

2½ oz/75 g cold butter, cut into
   pieces

cold water

FILLING

2 pieces or ¼ oz/6 g fine leaf gelatin

cold water

seeds of 8 cardamom pods

12 oz/350 g white chocolate, chopped
   into small pieces

generous 1½ cups whipping cream

White Chocolate and Cardamom Tart

You could serve this tart decorated with white chocolate curls or simply sift a little unsweetened cocoa over the white chocolate before serving. Edible flower petals sprinkled over the surface make a pretty decoration, too.

• Lightly grease a 9-inch/22-cm loose-bottom fluted tart pan. Sift the flour and salt into a food processor, add the butter, and process until the mixture resembles fine bread crumbs. Tip the mixture into a large bowl and add a little cold water, just enough to bring the dough together. Turn out onto a counter dusted with more flour and roll out the dough 3¼ inches/8 cm larger than the pan. Carefully lift the dough into the pan and press to fit. Roll the rolling pin over the pan to neaten the edges and trim the excess dough. Fit a piece of parchment paper into the tart shell, fill with dried beans, and let chill for 30 minutes. Meanwhile, preheat the oven to 375°F/190°C.

• Remove the pastry shell from the refrigerator and bake blind for 15 minutes in the preheated oven, then remove the beans and paper and bake for an additional 10 minutes. Let cool completely.

• Soak the gelatin in a little cold water in a small heatproof bowl for 5 minutes. Heat a pan of water to simmering point. Crush the cardamom seeds until powdery and put in a large bowl with the chocolate. Place the bowl of gelatin over the pan of simmering water and stir until dissolved. At the same time, in a separate pan, heat the cream until just boiling, then pour over the chocolate, using a whisk to stir the chocolate until it has melted. Add the gelatin and stir until the mixture is smooth. Let cool and pour into the tart shell, then let chill for at least 3 hours.

SERVES 6
PIE DOUGH
generous ¾ cup all-purpose flour
pinch of salt
2½ oz/75 g cold butter, cut into
    pieces
cold water

FILLING
10½ oz/300 g marzipan
1⅝ cups ground almonds
5½ oz/150 g unsalted butter
½ cup superfine sugar
scant ½ cup all-purpose flour
2 eggs

½ cup golden raisins
scant ⅓ cup mixed candied
    peel, chopped
scant ½ cup natural candied
    cherries, halved
½ cup slivered almonds

Sicilian Marzipan Tart with Candied Fruit

Serve warm with light cream or whisk a little almond liqueur and confectioners' sugar into mascarpone cheese. Sicilian dessert wine is delicious with this tart.

• Lightly grease a 9-inch/22-cm loose-bottom fluted tart pan. Sift the flour and salt into a food processor, add the butter, and process until the mixture resembles fine bread crumbs. Tip the mixture into a large bowl and add a little cold water, just enough to bring the dough together. Turn out onto a counter dusted with more flour and roll out the dough 3¼ inches/8 cm larger than the pan. Carefully lift the dough into the pan and press to fit. Roll the rolling pin over the pan to neaten the edges and trim the excess dough. Fit a piece of parchment paper into the tart shell, fill with dried beans, and let chill for 30 minutes. Meanwhile, preheat the oven to 375°F/190°C.

• Remove the pastry shell from the refrigerator and bake blind for 10 minutes in the preheated oven, then remove the beans and paper and bake for an additional 5 minutes.

• Lower the oven temperature to 350°F/180°C. Grate the marzipan straight onto the base of the warm dough, distributing evenly. Put the ground almonds, butter, and sugar in a food processor and pulse until smooth. Add 1 tbsp flour and 1 of the eggs and blend, then add another 1 tbsp flour and the other egg and blend. Finally add the remaining flour. Scoop the mixture into a bowl and stir in the golden raisins, peel, and cherries. Spoon the mixture over the marzipan, sprinkle with the slivered almonds, and bake for 40 minutes.

SERVES 6

PIE DOUGH

generous ¾ cup all-purpose flour

pinch of salt

2½ oz/75 g cold butter, cut into
    pieces

cold water

FILLING

⅔ cup brandy or Armagnac

½ cup golden superfine sugar

4–5 ripe but not soft plums, halved

1 whole egg, plus 2 egg yolks

1¼ cups heavy cream

Brandied Plum Tart

This tart is easily adapted. Use cherries, apricots, or stewed rhubarb if you don't want to use plums. You could also use a fruit compote or homemade jelly.

• Lightly grease a 9-inch/22-cm loose-bottom fluted tart pan. Sift the flour and salt into a food processor, add the butter, and process until the mixture resembles fine bread crumbs. Tip the mixture into a large bowl and add a little cold water, just enough to bring the dough together. Turn out onto a counter dusted with more flour and roll out the dough 3¼ inches/8 cm larger than the pan. Carefully lift the dough into the pan and press to fit. Roll the rolling pin over the pan to neaten the edges and trim the excess dough. Fit a piece of parchment paper into the tart shell, fill with dried beans, and let chill for 30 minutes. Meanwhile, preheat the oven to 375°F/190°C.

• Remove the pastry shell from the refrigerator and bake blind for 10 minutes in the preheated oven, then remove the beans and paper and bake for an additional 5 minutes.

• Put the brandy and 2 tbsp of the sugar in a pan and bring to a simmer, making sure the sugar has dissolved. Add the plum halves and let simmer for 5 minutes, then let cool. Lower the oven temperature to 325°F/160°C.

• Lift the plums out of the syrup with a slotted spoon, reserving the syrup. Slip the skins off the plums and slice each half plum into 3–4 slices, arranging the slices in the base of the pastry shell. Beat the egg and the egg yolks with the remaining sugar and heat the cream until just boiling. Whisk the hot cream into the eggs, stirring constantly. Spoon the filling over the plums, return the tart to the oven, and cook for 30–40 minutes, until the filling is set. Leave in the pan until completely cold, then carefully lift onto a serving plate. Serve with the reserved syrup in a small pitcher to drizzle over.

MAKES 6 TARTLETS

PRALINE

½ cup sugar

3 tbsp water

scant ½ cup slivered almonds

butter

PIE DOUGH

generous ¾ cup all-purpose flour

pinch of salt

2½ oz/75 g cold butter, cut
    into pieces

1 tsp confectioners' sugar

cold water

FRANGIPANE

2½ oz/75 g butter

2 eggs

generous ⅓ cup superfine sugar

2 tbsp all-purpose flour

1 cup ground almonds

TOPPING

8 natural candied cherries, chopped

2 tbsp mixed candied peel, chopped

3½ oz/100 g semisweet chocolate,
    chopped

Florentine Praline Tartlets

You can substitute white
or milk chocolate for the
semisweet chocolate or
use dried figs or apricots
instead of the candied peel.
A little chopped preserved
ginger is also very good
added to the topping.

• First make the praline. Put the sugar and the water in a pan and dissolve the sugar over low heat. Do not stir the sugar, just let it boil for 10 minutes, until it turns to caramel, then stir in the nuts and turn out onto buttered foil. Let cool and harden. When cold break up the praline and chop into smallish pieces.

• Grease 6 x 3½-inch/9-cm loose-bottom fluted tart pans. Sift the flour and salt into a food processor, add the butter, and process until the mixture resembles fine bread crumbs. Tip the mixture into a large bowl, add the sugar, and a little cold water, just enough to bring the dough together. Turn out onto a floured counter and divide into 6 equal-size pieces. Roll each piece to fit the tart pans. Carefully fit each piece of dough in its shell and press well to fit the pan. Roll the rolling pin over the pan to neaten the edges and trim the excess dough. Put in the freezer for 30 minutes. Meanwhile, preheat the oven to 400°F/200°C.

• While the tarts are in the freezer, make the frangipane. Melt the butter and beat the eggs and sugar together. Stir the melted butter into the egg and sugar mixture, then add the flour and almonds. Bake the tart shells blind, straight from the freezer, for 10 minutes in the preheated oven. Divide the frangipane between the tart shells and return to the oven for 8–10 minutes. Let cool completely.

• While the tarts are baking, mix the cherries, peel, chocolate, and praline together. Divide between the tarts while they are still hot so that some of the chocolate melts. Serve cold.

MAKES 6 TARTLETS
PIE DOUGH
generous ¾ cup all-purpose flour
pinch of salt
2½ oz/75 g cold butter, cut into
    pieces
1 tsp confectioners' sugar
cold water

COMPOTE
1 lb 2 oz/500 g fresh strawberries,
    hulled and quartered
1 tsp superfine sugar or 1 tsp flower
    honey
1 tsp orange flower water (optional)

FILLING
1 vanilla bean
¼ cup superfine sugar
generous 1 cup heavy cream
1½ pieces or ⅓ oz/4 g leaf gelatin
cold water
confectioners' sugar, to serve

Panna Cotta Tartlets with Strawberry Compote

Fresh fruit compote can be made by adding a little honey or sugar to berries or sliced pitted fruits such as peaches, apricots, or plums, adding a little complementary liquor, and simmering until soft. Let chill until needed.

• Grease 6 x 3½-inch/9-cm loose-bottom fluted tart pans. Sift the flour and salt into a food processor, add the butter, and process until the mixture resembles fine bread crumbs. Tip the mixture into a large bowl, add the sugar, and a little cold water, just enough to bring the dough together. Turn out onto a floured counter and divide into 6 equal-size pieces. Roll each piece to fit the tartlet pans. Carefully fit each piece of dough in its shell and press well to fit the pan. Roll the rolling pin over the pan to neaten the edges and trim the excess dough. Put in the freezer for 30 minutes. Meanwhile, preheat the oven to 400°F/200°C. Bake the tart shells blind, straight from the freezer, for 15 minutes in the preheated oven. Cool the tart shells completely, carefully remove from the pans, and transfer to a serving plate.

• To make the compote, heat the strawberries in a pan with the sugar or honey and flower water (if using). When the fruits start to break down, lower the heat, and let simmer for 2–3 minutes. Let cool completely.

• To make the filling, split the vanilla bean lengthwise and put into a pan with the sugar and half the cream. Bring gently to a simmer. Meanwhile, soak the gelatin in a little cold water. When the cream is very hot remove the vanilla bean, lift the gelatin from the water, and stir into the cream until completely dissolved. Scrape the vanilla seeds into the warm cream and stir again. Let cool. (Wipe the vanilla bean dry and use in another recipe.)

• Whisk the remaining cream until it starts to thicken, then fold the creams together. Let chill until cold, spoon into the pastry shells, and let chill for 2 hours. When ready to serve, spoon the strawberry compote onto the tarts, and sift a little confectioners' sugar on top.

SERVES 6

PIE DOUGH

1⅛ cups all-purpose flour

pinch of salt

3½ oz/100 g cold butter, cut
    into pieces

2 tbsp superfine sugar

1 egg yolk

cold water

FILLING

5 lemons

2 eggs

1½ cups superfine sugar

generous 1½ cups ground almonds

generous ⅓ cup whipping cream

generous ⅓ cup water

Caramelized Lemon Tart

The ground almonds in the filling make this a rather substantial tart, quite different from the smooth-textured classic French Tarte au Citron. The sticky lemon slices on the top mean this tart will not slice neatly—but it is so delicious that no one will mind.

• Lightly grease a 9-inch/22-cm loose-bottom fluted tart pan. Sift the flour and salt into a food processor, add the butter, and process until the mixture resembles fine bread crumbs. Tip the mixture into a large bowl, add the sugar and egg yolk, and a little cold water, just enough to bring the dough together. Turn out onto a counter dusted with more flour and roll out the dough 3¼ inches/8 cm larger than the pan. Carefully lift the dough into the pan and press to fit. Roll the rolling pin over the pan to neaten the edges and trim the excess dough. Fit a piece of parchment paper into the tart shell, fill with dried beans, and let chill in the refrigerator for 30 minutes. Meanwhile, preheat the oven to 375°F/190°C.

• Remove the pastry shell from the refrigerator and bake blind for 10 minutes in the preheated oven, then remove the beans and paper and bake for an additional 5 minutes.

• Put the juice and finely grated rind of 3 of the lemons in a large bowl and add the eggs, ½ cup of the sugar, the ground almonds, and the cream, whisking to combine. Pour into the pastry shell and bake for 25 minutes. Meanwhile, thinly slice the remaining 2 lemons, discarding the seeds and ends. Put the remaining sugar and water in a pan and heat until the sugar is melted. Let simmer for 5 minutes, then add the lemon slices and boil for 10 minutes.

• Remove the tart from the oven and arrange the lemon slices over the surface in a spiral pattern. Drizzle the remaining lemon syrup over the slices. Serve warm or cold, with whipped cream.

SERVES 6

PIE DOUGH

generous ¾ cup all-purpose flour

pinch of salt

2½ oz/75 g cold butter, cut into
    pieces

cold water

FILLING

2 lb 4 oz/1 kg canned sweetened
    chestnut purée

1¼ cups heavy cream

2 tbsp butter

2 tbsp maple syrup

1 cup pecans

Chestnut, Maple Syrup, and Pecan Tart

This tart is very rich and sweet. If you would prefer it less sweet, replace half of the sweetened chestnut purée with unsweetened, and add maple syrup to taste until the mixture is the sweetness you like.

• Lightly grease a 9-inch/22-cm loose-bottom fluted tart pan. Sift the flour and salt into a food processor, add the butter, and process until the mixture resembles fine bread crumbs. Tip the mixture into a large bowl and add a little cold water, just enough to bring the dough together. Turn out onto a counter dusted with more flour and roll out the dough 3¼ inches/8 cm larger than the pan. Carefully lift the dough into the pan and press to fit. Roll the rolling pin over the pan to neaten the edges and trim the excess dough. Fit a piece of parchment paper into the tart shell, fill with dried beans, and let chill in the refrigerator for 30 minutes. Meanwhile, preheat the oven to 375°F/190°C.

• Remove the shell from the refrigerator and bake for 15 minutes, then remove the beans and paper and bake for an additional 10 minutes.

• Empty the chestnut purée into a large bowl. Whip the cream until stiff and fold into the chestnut purée. Spoon into the cold pastry shell and let chill for 2 hours. Melt the butter with the maple syrup and when bubbling add the pecans and stir for 1–2 minutes. Spoon onto parchment paper and let cool. When ready to serve, arrange the pecans on the chestnut cream.

SERVES 6

PIE DOUGH

generous ¾ cup all-purpose flour

pinch of salt

2½ oz/75 g cold butter, cut into
   pieces

1 egg yolk

finely grated rind of ½ orange

cold water

FILLING

3 tbsp orange marmalade

1 egg, plus 3 egg yolks

½ cup superfine sugar

generous 1½ cups heavy cream

finely grated rind of 1 orange and the
   juice of ½ orange

½ tsp orange flower water (optional)

TO DECORATE

finely grated orange rind

confectioners' sugar

Orange Marmalade Tart

Instead of the orange flower water you can use Cointreau or another orange-flavored liqueur and serve a glass of it with the tart along with some chilled light cream.

• Lightly grease a 9-inch/22-cm loose-bottom fluted tart pan. Sift the flour and salt into a food processor, add the butter, and process until the mixture resembles fine bread crumbs. Tip the mixture into a large bowl, add the egg yolk and orange rind, and a little cold water, just enough to bring the dough together. Turn out onto a counter dusted with more flour and roll out the dough 3¼ inches/8 cm larger than the pan. Carefully lift the dough into the pan and press to fit. Roll the rolling pin over the pan to neaten the edges and trim the excess dough. Fit a piece of parchment paper into the tart shell, fill with dried beans, and let chill in the refrigerator for 30 minutes. Preheat the oven to 375°F/190°C.

• Remove the pastry shell from the refrigerator and bake blind for 10 minutes in the preheated oven, then remove the beans and paper and bake for an additional 5 minutes.

• Lower the oven temperature to 325°F/160°C. Spread the marmalade over the base of the pastry shell. Beat the egg, egg yolks, and sugar together and heat the cream until simmering. Pour the hot cream over the egg mixture, whisking to combine, then add the orange rind, orange juice, and orange flower water (if using) and stir well. Pour on top of the marmalade and bake for 40–45 minutes. Serve cold.

Index

almonds
  ground 68, 73, 82, 91
  slivered 70, 82, 86
amaretti cookies 75
anchovies 16, 46
apple galette with applejack
  cream 70
applejack brandy 70, 73
apples 52, 56, 70
apricots 52, 85, 86, 88
artichoke and pancetta tartlets 22

balsamic duck and radicchio
  tartlets 14
balsamic vinegar 32
bell peppers 10, 22, 32
berries 51, 54, 59, 60, 75, 88
blackberries 51
bleu cheese and walnut tartlets 18
blueberries 59
bramble tart with cassis cream 51
brandied plum tart 85

candied fruit 82
caramelized lemon tart 91
cardamom 80
cassis 51, 59, 60
Catalan pimiento tartlets 10
cherries 75, 82, 85, 86
cherry tomato and poppy seed
  tartlets 16
chestnut, maple syrup, and pecan
  tart 92
chocolate
  dessert tarts 75, 77, 80, 86
  pie dough 60, 77
chorizo 10
coconut 54, 66
crab and watercress tart 30
cream cheese 16, 78
curd cheese 78
curried onion tart 43

dessert tarts
  fruit 48–73
  rich 74–95

dill 13
duck and radicchio tartlets 14

eggplant, pesto, and prosciutto
  tartlets 26
eggs 7, 21, 59, 75
elderberry 62
exotic fruits 49, 54, 65, 66

feta and spinach tartlets 24
fig, ricotta, and honey tart 68
fine chocolate tart 77
Florentine praline tartlets 86
fontina 35

ginger 56, 86
goat cheese and thyme tart 46
Gorgonzola 35, 36
Gruyère 44

haddock, smoked, and Gruyère
  soufflé tart 44
ham 21, 22, 26, 44
honey 68, 78
horseradish 13

individual tarts 8–27, 42, 75

jewel berry tart 60

leeks 18, 40
lemon 59, 91
lemon curd and blueberry tart 59
lemon grass and mango tart 54

main course tarts 28–47
mango 54, 66
maple syrup 92
Marsala 73
marzipan tart with candied fruit 82
mascarpone cheese 82
mozzarella cheese 22, 26

olives 22, 35, 46
onions 14, 35, 38, 40, 43
orange marmalade tart 94

pancetta 22
panna cotta tarts with strawberry
  compote 88
Parmesan 16, 21, 22, 30, 38, 40
passion fruit brûlée tart 65
pea, ham, and sour cream
  tartlets 21
peach and preserved ginger tarte
  tatin 56
peaches 51, 56, 88
pear, poached, with Marsala
  syllabub 73
pears 52, 56, 73
peas 40
pecans 18, 92
pesto 22, 26
pimiento tartlets, Catalan 10
pine nuts 24, 32
plums 51, 56, 85, 88
poached pear tart with Marsala
  syllabub 73
pomegranate 60
poppy seeds 16
potato, fontina and rosemary
  tart 35
praline 86
prosciutto 26
pumpkin 36

quince 49, 52

radicchio 14, 46
raspberries 51, 75
rhubarb 85
ricotta 68
rosemary 35

sage 36
salami 32
salmon 30
salmon, smoked, dill and
  horseradish tartlets 13
Sicilian marzipan tart with candied
  fruit 82
sour cream 13, 21, 77
spinach 24

spring vegetable tart 40
squash, sage, and Gorgonzola
  tart 36
strawberries 51, 62, 88
strawberry and elderberry tart 62
syllabub, Marsala 73

tarte tatin 56
thyme 46
toffee apple tart 52
tomato 16, 32
triple tomato tart 32
tropical fruit tart 66
truffled honey tart 78

walnuts 18, 46
watercress
white chocolate and cardamom
  tart 80

yellow zucchini tart 38

zucchini, yellow 38